# Take Care of Yourself

# Staying Safe in the Sun

## Siân Smith

**www.raintreepublishers.co.uk**
Visit our website to find out more information about Raintree books.

**To order:**
☎ Phone 0845 6044371
🖷 Fax +44 (0) 1865 312263
🖳 Email myorders@raintreepublishers.co.uk

Customers from outside the UK please telephone +44 1865 312262

Raintree is an imprint of Capstone Global Library Limited, a company incorporated in England and Wales having its registered office at 7 Pilgrim Street, London, EC4V 6LB– Registered company number: 6695582

Edited by Dan Nunn, Rebecca Rissman, and John-Paul Wilkins
Designed by Victoria Allen
Picture research by Tracy Cummins
Production by Alison Parsons
Originated by Capstone Global Library Ltd
Printed and bound in China by Leo Paper Products Ltd

ISBN 978 1 406 24162 4
16 15 14 13 12
10 9 8 7 6 5 4 3 2 1

**British Library Cataloguing in Publication Data**
Smith, Siân.
Staying safe in the sun. – (Take care of yourself)
613.1'13-dc22
A full catalogue record for this book is available from the British Library.

**Acknowledgements**
We would like to thank the following for permission to reproduce photographs: Capstone Library pp. 15, 23b (Karon Dubke); Corbis pp. 11, 12, 23c (© Randy Faris); Dreamstime.com p. 22a (© Hunk); Getty Images p. 16 (Photolibrary); istockphoto pp. 6 (© Joel Carillet), 9 (© Jo Ann Snover), 14, 22d (© mark wragg), 18 (© Wilson Valentin), 19 (© Linda Epstein), 20 (© Marilyn Nieves); Shutterstock pp. 4 (© holbox), 5 (© Yuriy Kulyk), 7 (© AISPIX), 8 (© Rob Marmion), 10 (© Dubova), 13, 17 (© MaszaS), 21, 23a (© wavebreakmedia ltd), 22b (© Teeratas), 22c (© Marek R. Swadzba).

Front cover photograph of Hispanic mother rubbing sunscreen on daughter at beach reproduced with permission of Getty Images (Erik Isakson). Rear cover photograph of family on cruise ship reproduced with permission of Shutterstock (© Rob Marmion).

Every effort has been made to contact copyright holders of material reproduced in this book. Any omissions will be rectified in subsequent printings if notice is given to the publisher.

We would like to thank Nancy Harris and Dee Reid for their assistance in the preparation of this book.

# Contents

# Sunshine

A little bit of sunshine is good for our bodies.

But the sun is hot and powerful.

Too much sunshine can hurt our bodies.

You can have fun in the sun, but
you must stay safe in it, too.

# Keep your eyes safe

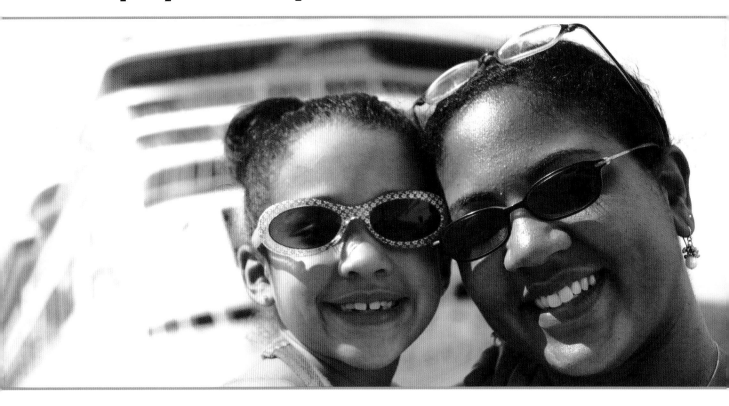

On sunny days wear sunglasses
to keep your eyes safe.

Never look right at the sun,
even with sunglasses.

# On sunny days

On sunny days put suncream on your skin to keep it safe.

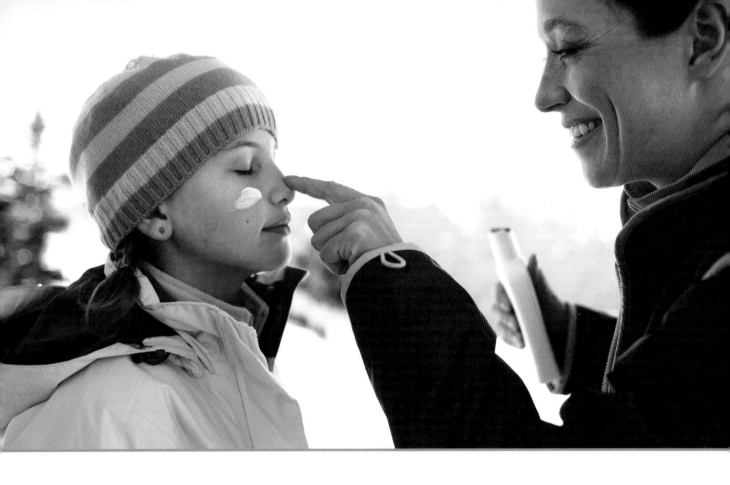

Don't forget your ears and
your nose!

Put on more cream after
a few hours.

If your cream washes off, put more on.

Suncreams with high numbers keep you safer.

Sunblock keeps your nose
and cheeks safe. It comes in
bright colours.

You can wear a top with sleeves to keep your arms safe.

You can wear white clothes to keep you cooler.

You can wear a hat to keep
your head safe.

There are lots of different hats
you can try.

When the weather is hot,
drink lots of water.

Don't stay in the sunshine too long.
Find some shade if you can.

# Name game

Can you name these things? They help you to stay safe in the sun.

Answers on page 24

# Picture glossary

 **shade**  cool place away from strong sunlight

 **sunblock**  special cream you use to block the sun. Some sunblock comes in bright colours.

 **suncream**  special cream you use to stay safe in the sun

# Index

---

**Answers to question on page 22**

a = white top    b = sunglasses

c = hat    d = suncream

---

**Notes for parents and teachers**

**Before reading**

Talk with the children about different ways of keeping our bodies safe. Find out what they know about staying safe in the sun. What do they do to keep their bodies safe? Bring in or show them pictures of different factor suncreams. Do they know what the numbers mean? Explain that suncreams with higher numbers give us more protection from the sun.

**After reading**

• With the children, list all the things you can do to help you to stay safe in the sun with the children. Play a memory game in groups. Start the game by saying "When I go out in the sun I..." and then choose a way of staying safe in the sun. For example you could wear sunglasses, wear suncream, wear sunblock, wear a hat, move to the shade when hot, or drink lots of water. Take turns to repeat what has been said so far and to add another way of staying safe in the sun.

• Reinforce techniques for staying safe in the sun by helping the children to design posters that show others how to stay safe. If a digital camera is available, children could take photos of items that help them to stay safe, to use in their posters.